EVERYTHING ORIGAMI

ORIGAMI TOYS

MATTHEW GARDINER

**WINDMILL
BOOKS**
New York

Symbols

Lines

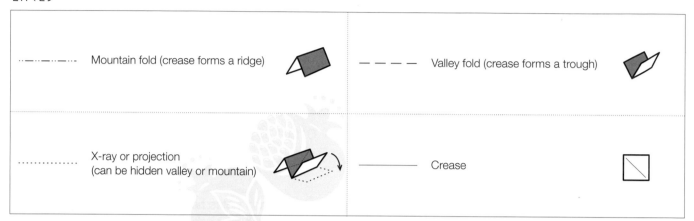

·–··–··–··–	Mountain fold (crease forms a ridge)		— — — —	Valley fold (crease forms a trough)
·············	X-ray or projection (can be hidden valley or mountain)		————	Crease

Arrows

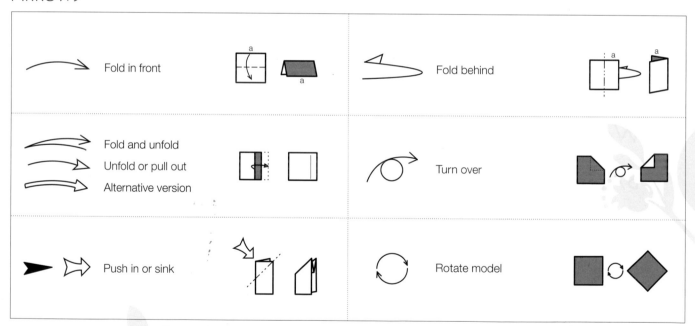

Fold in front

Fold behind

Fold and unfold
Unfold or pull out
Alternative version

Turn over

Push in or sink

Rotate model

Extras

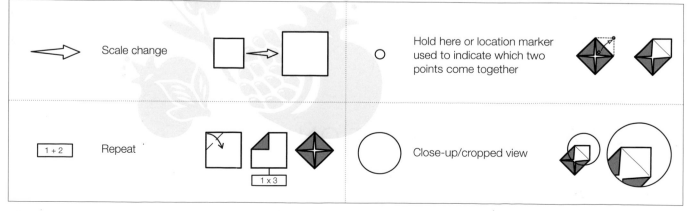

Scale change

○ Hold here or location marker used to indicate which two points come together

1 + 2   Repeat

Close-up/cropped view

TYPES OF FOLDS

BOOK FOLD   Valley fold one edge to another, like closing a book.

CUPBOARD FOLD 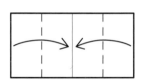 Fold both edges to the middle crease, like closing two cupboard doors.

BLINTZ   Fold all corners to the middle. This was named after a style of pastry called a blintz.

PLEAT   A mountain and valley fold combination.

BISECT –

DIVIDE A POINT IN TWO    Many folds use a corner and two edges to position the fold line. The most common is a bisection, or division of an angle in two.

Fold one edge to meet the other, making sure the crease goes through the corner.

INSIDE REVERSE FOLD   The spine of the existing fold is reversed and pushed inside.

OUTSIDE REVERSE FOLD

The spine of the existing fold is reversed and wrapped outside.

DOUBLE REVERSE

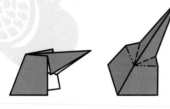

A double reverse fold is two reverse folds made in sequence on the same point.

The last diagram shows the paper slightly unfolded, to illustrate the folds that are made.

INSIDE CRIMP   ## OUTSIDE CRIMP

Crimps are often used for making feet or shaping legs. They can be thought of as a pleat mirrored on both sides of the point.

An inside crimp tucks the pleat on the inside of the point.

An outside crimp wraps the pleat over the outside of the point.

PETAL FOLD   The petal fold is found in the bird and lily base.

1   2   3   4   5

Fold top layer to the center crease.

Fold and unfold the top triangle down. Unfold flaps.

Lift the top layer upwards.

Step 3 in progress, the model is 3D. Fold the top layer inwards on existing creases.

Completed petal fold.

SQUASH   A squash fold is the symmetrical flattening of a point. The flattening movement is known as squashing the point.

1   2   3   4

Pre-crease on the line for the squash fold.

Open up the paper by inserting your finger. Fold the paper across.

As you put the paper in place, gently squash the point into a symmetrical shape.

Completed squash fold.

OPEN SINK

1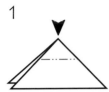

Pre crease through all layers along the sink line. It's best to make a mountain and a valley fold on this line.

2

Open out the point, and push the point into the paper. Take care to reverse folds as shown. The sink should squash flat.

3

Completed sink.

RABBIT EAR The rabbit ear fold is named after a most useful shape – that of a rabbit ear. It is used to make a new point.

1   2   3   4   5   6

1-3. Divide each corner of the triangle with valley folds.

Fold top edges to the bottom, the middle crease will form a point.

Fold the point to one side.

Completed rabbit ear.

DOUBLE RABBIT EAR The double rabbit ear is a rabbit ear fold that is mirrored on both sides of the point.

1   2   3   4   5   6

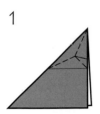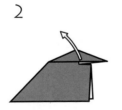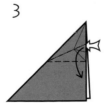

Make a rabbit ear fold on the point.

Unfold the rabbit ear.

Squash fold the point.

Inside reverse fold the two points.

Valley fold point upwards.

Completed double rabbit ear.

SWIVEL FOLD

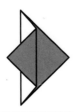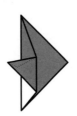

A swivel fold is often made on a pleat. It narrows its two points, and the excess paper swivels under one of the points.

FLAPPING BIRD

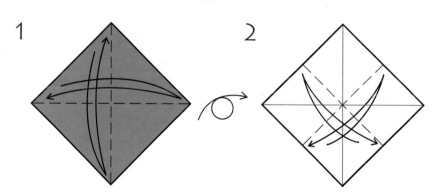

The flapping bird is a variation of the paper crane. This variation has a beautiful mechanism that pulls the paper of the wings, causing them to flap. There are a few varieties of flapping birds – this one is the original and a classic.

The smallest flapping bird in the world was folded by Akira Naito in Japan. His smallest ever model so far is a paper crane folded from a 0.0039 inch (0.1mm) square, using plastic film instead of paper, a microscope and special handmade micro origami tools.

1

Start colored side up.
Fold and unfold diagonals.
Turn over.

2

Book fold and unfold.

3

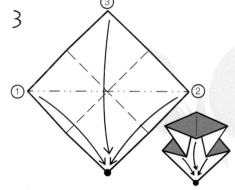

Bring three corners down to meet bottom corner. Start with corners 1 and 2 together followed by corner 3.

4

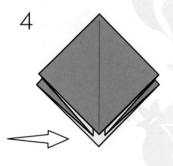

Completed preliminary base.

5

Fold top layer to the center crease.

6

Fold the top triangle down and unfold.
Unfold flaps.

7

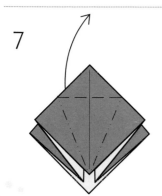

Lift the top layer upwards.

8

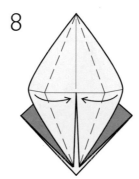

Step 7 in progress, the model is 3D. Fold the top layer inwards on existing creases.

9

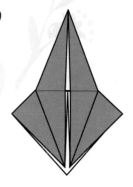

Step 7 completed, the model will be flat. Turn over.

10

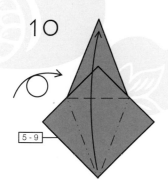

5 - 9

Repeat steps 5-9 on this side.

11

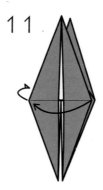

Turn front and back flap over.

12

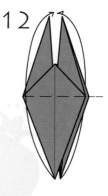

Fold flaps up.

13

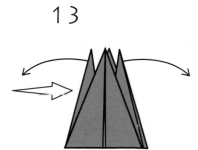

Swivel the two points outwards. These form the head and tail.

14

The next steps show details of forming the head.

15

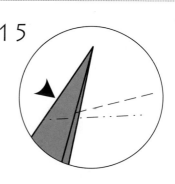

Reverse fold.

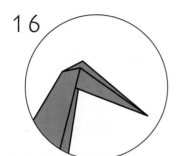

16

Step 15 completed.

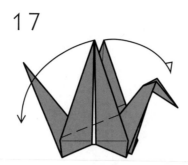

17

Fold down wings. Make soft folds.

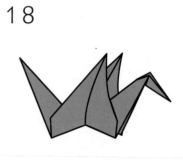

18

Completed flapping bird.

19

To make the bird flap hold the model at the black dots. Gently pull on the tail and the wings will flap down. Gently release and the wings will go back up. Repeat.

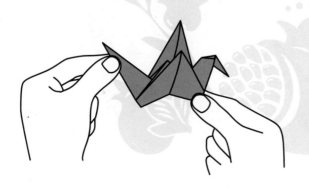

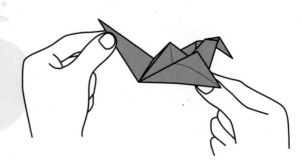

DRINKING BIRD

The drinking bird is a well-known toy, a bird that drinks the water and keeps drinking by itself. This origami model is a little different – the bird does drink, but you have to help it.

The drinking bird has a pool, and a very interesting origami mechanism that pushes its head forwards as you push upwards.

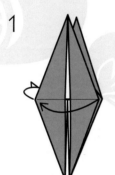

1

Start from the bird base (Step 11, on page 9). Turn front and back flap over.

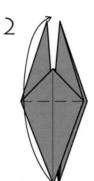

2

Move top layer up.

3

Fold down.

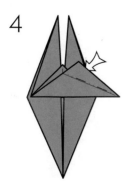

4

Reverse fold top layer. Steps 3-4 are a different way to make a rabbit ear fold.

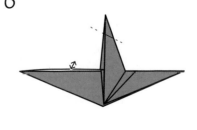

5

Rotate 90°. Mountain fold the model in half. Allow the top layer to flip up.

6

To form the head, inside reverse fold. Widen out drinking trough.

7

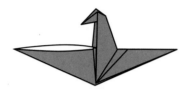

Completed drinking bird.

8

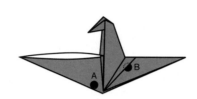

To make the bird drink hold the trough in one hand (at point A) and slip your fingers inside the pockets at point B and move your fingers up and down.

9

Allow the layers of paper under the neck, as shown by the darkened area, to become loose. As you push up, the bird's neck will dip forward and drink.

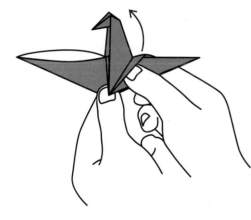

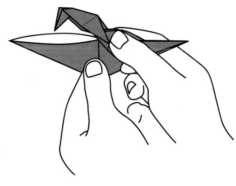

BOAT

The boat is a fantastic origami model. At step 9 the model forms a hat and by step 14 you have an origami model that actually floats. For longer floating time, use a greaseproof paper, or better yet, modern technology has produced synthetic paper that won't soak up water, so your boat won't sink.

A German artist named Frank Bölter has used this origami design, with special paper and lots of help, to actually sail down rivers in Europe!

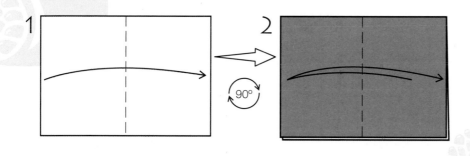

1

Start with a rectangle. Letter (8.5 x 11 in) is a good size – use a sheet of newspaper for a wearable hat. Book fold.

2

Turn 90° and book fold and unfold again.

3

Fold corners down.

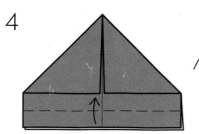

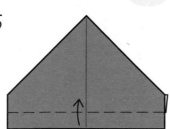

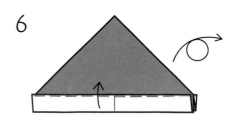

4

Fold up to the bottom of the triangles. Turn over.

5

Fold up to match the fold in step 4.

6

Fold up over the bottom of the triangle. Turn over.

7

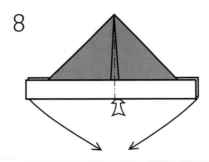

Repeat step 6.

8

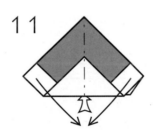

Lift the middle and push both points together, to make a squash fold.

9

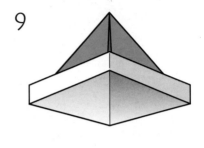

Squash fold in progress. This stage can also be used as a hat.

10

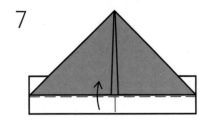

Repeat

Fold bottom point about one third. Repeat behind.

11

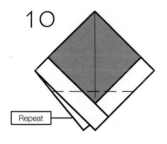

Squash fold, lifting the middle, similar to step 8.

12

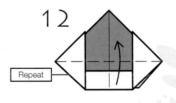

Repeat

Fold up. Repeat behind.

13

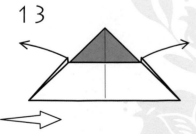

Pull the points out to shape the boat. The boat will become 3D.

14

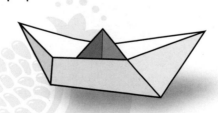

Completed boat.

WATER BOMB

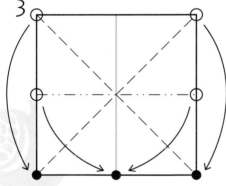

The water bomb is a classic because in the last move you actually get to inflate it! The model forms a box that can hold a liquid. Ironically, the water bomb, when made from paper, does not actually hold water for very long. Use plastic or greaseproof paper to keep the water a little longer.

Australian composer David Young wrote "16 Boxes," a musical piece for percussion with origami accompaniment. To perform this, the artist must fold 16 origami boxes (waterbombs) in 12 minutes: that's 45 seconds each.

1

Begin colored side up.
Book fold and unfold. Turn over.

2

Fold and unfold diagonals.

3

Collapse on existing creases.

4

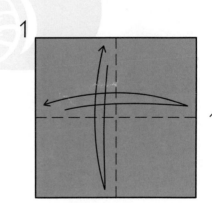

The waterbomb base.

5

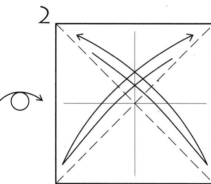

Fold corners up. Turn over.

6

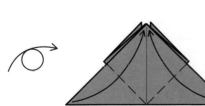

Repeat step 5.

THE WATER BOMB

7

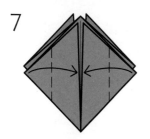

Fold corners of top layer to the middle.

8

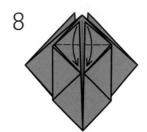

Fold top two flaps down.

9

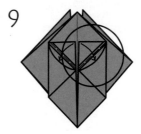

Pre-crease the triangles, and then tuck them into the pockets.

10

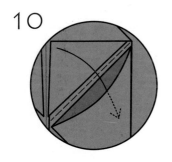

Detail of step 9, showing how to insert the triangle into the pocket.

11

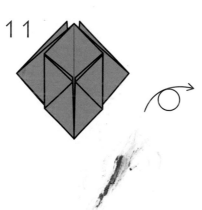

Step 9 completed. Turn over.

12

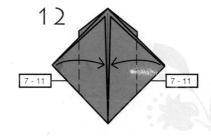

7 - 11   7 - 11

Repeat steps 7-11 on both sides.

13

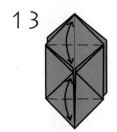

Fold and unfold top and bottom triangles.

14

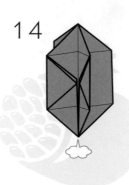

Pull flaps apart. Blow air into the hole in the bottom and shape into 3D cube.

15

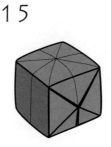

Completed water bomb.

GLIDER

Paper planes are one of the many wonders of the world. How can a sheet of paper and a few folds become a gravity-defying flying machine? This glider is a simple but stable model that flies well. If you curve the rear corners upwards a little, you accelerate lift, causing it to do loop-the-loops.

World record holder Ken Blackburn set his record of longest time aloft at the Georgia Dome in Atlanta in 1998. The record is 27.6 seconds of flight from a hand launch.

1

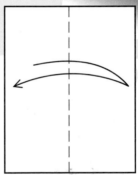

Use a letter (8.5 x 11 inch) sheet of paper. Book fold and unfold.

2

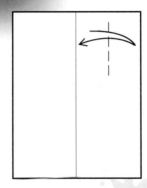

Fold and unfold edge to center crease. Make only a short crease as shown.

3

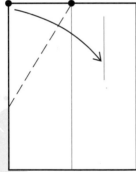

Fold the corner to touch the crease from step 2. Start the fold from the center crease.

4

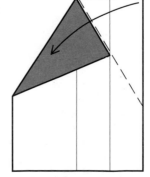

Fold other edge over.

5

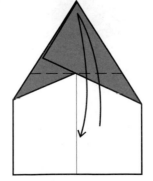

Fold across the intersection of the top layers, and unfold.

6

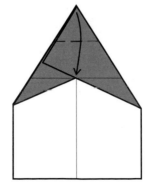

Fold to the previous crease.

7

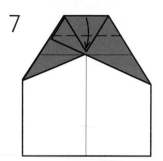

Fold the top edge to meet the intersection.

8

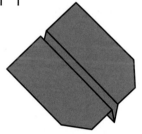

Fold over, and over again.

9

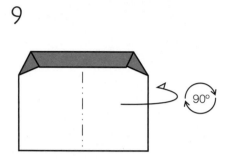

90°

Mountain fold in half.
Rotate 90°.

10

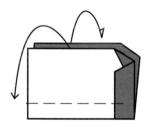

Fold both flaps down about 2 cm from the bottom.

11

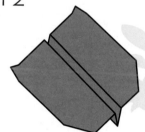

Completed glider.

12

Curve the back corners upwards. This will give the glider more lift, and allow you to do loop-the-loop tricks.

JUMPING FROG

The jumping frog is a paper racing game waiting to happen. All you need are a few friends and some jumping frogs and the game is on! High performance frogs can be made from card. Business cards make small dynamic frogs, but index cards are a more foldable size.

At the 2007 Australian Origami Convention, special guest Michael LaFosse used a secret racing frog design to win the Melbourne Paper Cup.

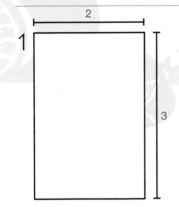

1

Choose a rectangle piece of paper with a ratio of 2:3. Index cards are a good size.

2

Begin white side up. Fold and unfold diagonally so that the top edge lines up with the side edge. Turn over.

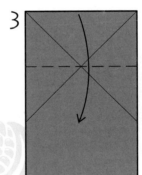

3

Fold and unfold through the crossing diagonals. Turn over.

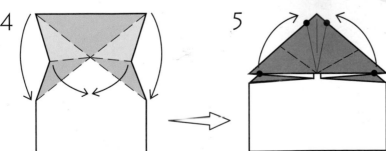

4

Fold top corners down. Fold midpoints inwards.

5

The top triangular shape is called a waterbomb base. Fold up the top two corners just short of the center line, so they point out a little.

6

Cupboard fold.

19

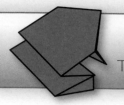

7

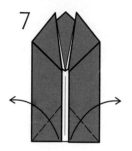

Fold out rear legs.

8

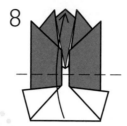

Fold in half, bringing the bottom to the top.

9

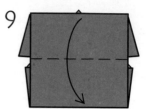

Fold the top layer in half, bringing the top to the bottom.

10

Turn the model over. Completed jumping frog.

11

To make the frog jump gently press and release at the point marked.

WALKING CRAB

The walking crab is a fun design that walks sideways when you tap it. Shoko is well known for her fun origami style – she likes to use stick-on eyes to add character to her origami creations. You cut out circles of white and black paper and glue them together, or use pre-cut circles that are available at office suppliers.

The walking crab is a contemporary Japanese design.

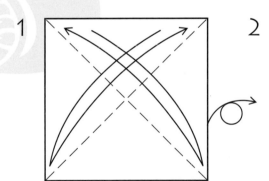

1

Fold and unfold diagonals. Turn over.

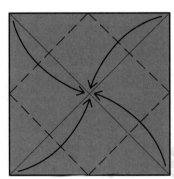

2

Blintz fold.

3

Completed step 2. Turn over.

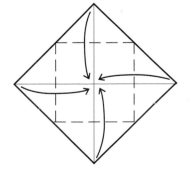

4

Blintz fold again.

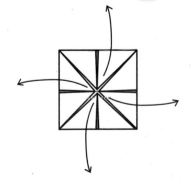

5

Completely unfold the paper.

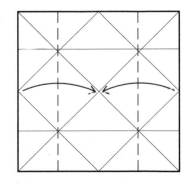

6

Then fold sides to center.

7

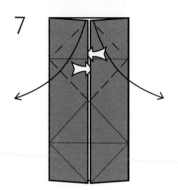

Bring both corners forwards
and squash fold.

8

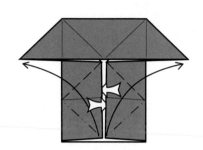

Repeat step 7 on other end.

9

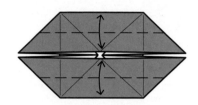

Fold and unfold top and bottom edge
to the center.

10

Open up pockets.

11

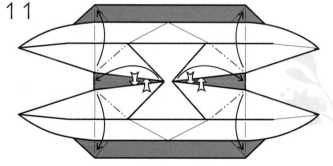

This shows the pockets open. Lift up inside
corners, and fold the edges outwards.

12

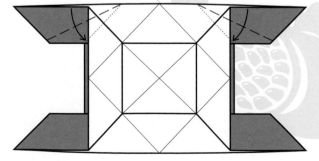

Fold edge to corner.

13

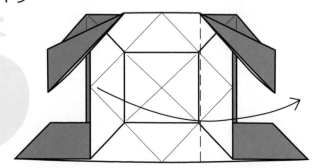

Fold over.

14

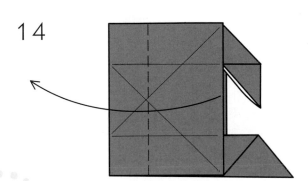

Fold over.

15

Fold in half through all layers.

16

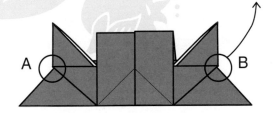

Hold "A" with one hand.
Pull "B" upwards.

17

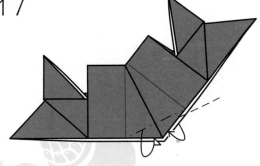

Fold inside the base of the front flap
as shown. Repeat on the other side.

18

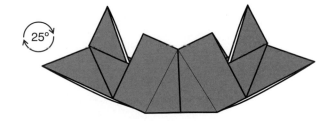

Completed walking crab.

19

When you tap the C, the crab will walk sideways.
Attach the round stickers for eyes and draw eyeballs.

BANGER

This single layer banger could be the alternative to shrill party whistles. It is best made from a sheet of newspaper.

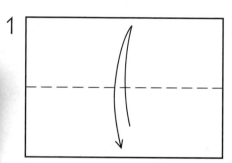

1

Start with a large thin rectangle. Newspaper works well. Book fold and unfold.

2

Fold corners over.

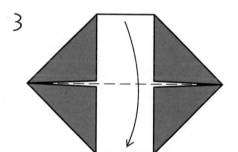

3

Fold in half.

4

Fold in half again.

5

Valley fold front and back points.

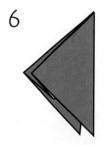

6

Completed banger.

BANG!

7

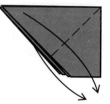

Hold at the points to use. To make a bang, thrust downwards.

FORTUNE TELLER

The fortune teller, also known as the "cootie catcher" or "salt cellar," is perhaps the best known origami game in the west. The game, played by children, uses colors and numbers to magically reveal the player's fortune.

The fortune teller is best made from a 12-inch (30 cm) square of white paper.

1

Fold and unfold diagonally.

2

Blintz fold. Turn over.

3

Blintz fold again.

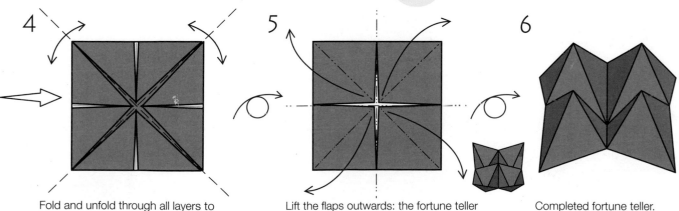

4

Fold and unfold through all layers to make the 3D opening process easier. Turn over.

5

Lift the flaps outwards: the fortune teller will become 3D. Turn over.

6

Completed fortune teller.

HOW TO PLAY:

DRAW

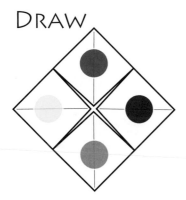

Flatten the model to step 5. Decorate your fortune teller with four colors.

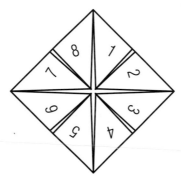

Turn over, and write the numbers from 1 to 8 on each of the triangles.

Open up all the points and write in your fortunes. Write one for each number.

MOVE

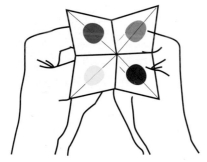

The "start" position. Thumbs and forefingers of both hands are together.

A

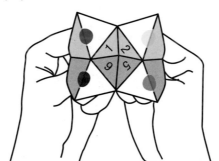

One count/letter. Thumbs and forefingers of each hand are together.

B

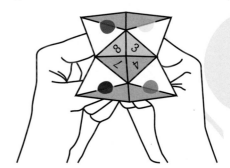

Next count. Both thumbs are together, and both forefingers are together.

PLAY

Begin in the "start" position.

Ask your friend to pick a color.

Spell out the color, letter by letter, and as you say each letter, alternate between the positions shown in A and B with the fortune teller, as shown above.

Ask your friend how many boyfriends/girlfriends they have, and count the number they say.

Ask your friend to pick a number. Unfold the flap that has the number, and read their fortune.

You can make up lots of fun fortunes.

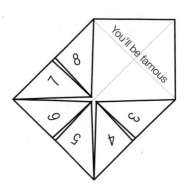

Fox

The fox is a cunning creature. In Japanese mythology, foxes possess magical abilities and wisdom, and some have the ability to change into human form. This fox is a fun little hand puppet that gives the wearer special fox abilities. Use this puppet with care, and respect the animals of the world.

The Japanese say that a sun-shower (rain falling from a clear sky) is the sign of a fox wedding.

1

Book fold and unfold.

2

Book fold.

3

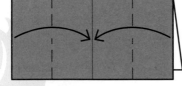

Cupboard fold.

4

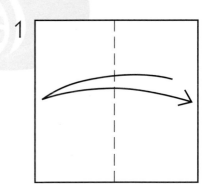

Open up the pocket and squash fold.

5

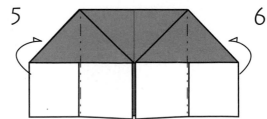

Mountain fold sides.

6

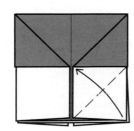

Fold up corner of top layer.

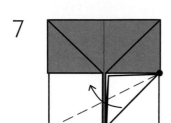

7

Fold up.

8

Fold up again.
Turn over.

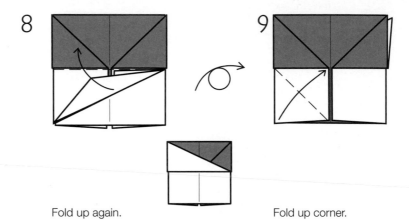

9

Fold up corner.

10

Fold up.

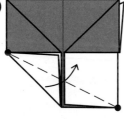

11

Fold up again.

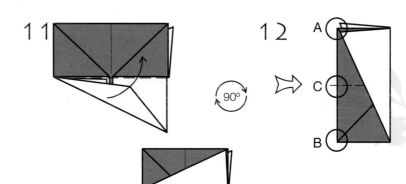

12

A

C

B

Push point C further in so point
A and B touch.

13

Completed fox.

14

Insert your hand in the back and
use as a puppet.

PUPPETS

This model can make two types of animal finger puppets – a cat and a pig. Fold them from a 6-inch (15 cm) square of paper, and carefully draw the faces on your puppets. Make a group of puppets and invent your own characters for these lovable creatures.

The art of puppetry is a rich tradition of storytelling, popular with both young and old.

1

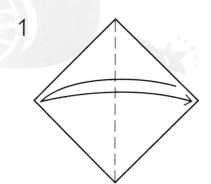

Fold and unfold diagonal.

2

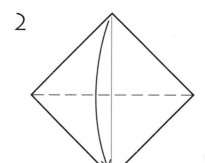

Fold in half diagonally.

3

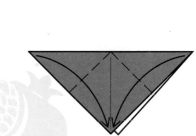

Fold side corners down to meet bottom corner.

4

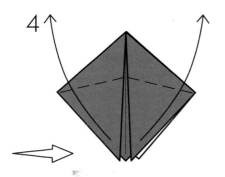

Fold two flaps up.

5

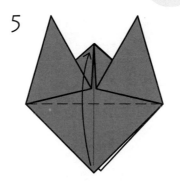

Fold top flap up.

6

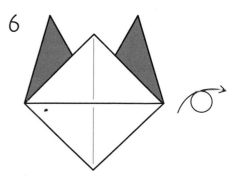

Fold top flap up. Turn over.

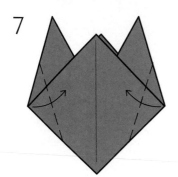

7

Fold corners in.

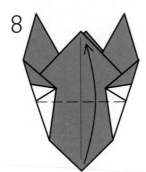

8

Fold up.

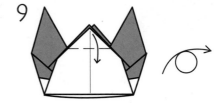

9

Fold all top layers down.
Turn over.

10

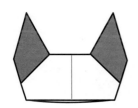

Completed cat face.

11

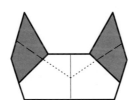

To make a pig face, fold ears over.

12

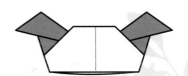

Completed pig face.

13

Draw a cat face and use as
a finger puppet.

14

Draw a pig face and use as
a finger puppet.

TALKER

The origami talker looks like a little mouth. There is a whole range of talking origami models, and this is perhaps one of the simplest and easiest to make.

The talker looks best when folded from a duo-toned paper.

1

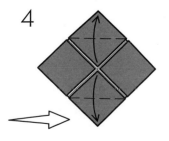

Book fold and unfold.

2

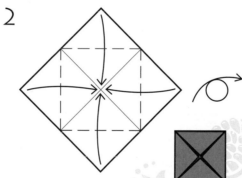

Blintz fold. Turn over.

3

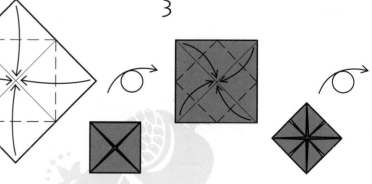

Blintz fold again. Turn over.

4

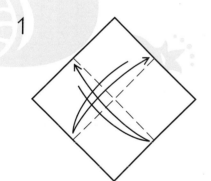

Fold top layer only.

5

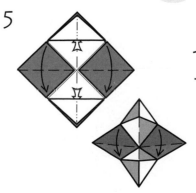

Poke your finger into the white pockets and lift up, then fold the model in half.

6

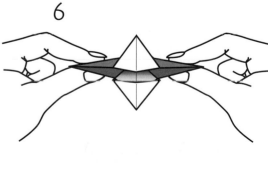

Completed talker. Hold as shown and push and pull the mouth together to make the talker talk.

Glossary

ACCELERATE to increase in speed

DYNAMIC producing an effect of energetic movement

FLAP to move up and down or back and forth

MECHANISM a structure of working parts functioning together

SYNTHETIC produced by artificial processes

VARIETY something differing from others

Index

For More Information

Ard, Catherine. *Origami on the Move*. New York: Gareth Stevens, 2015.

Owen, Rose. *More Halloween Origami*. New York: PowerKids Press, 2015.

For web resources related to the subject of this book, go to:
www.windmillbooks.com/weblinks and select this book's title.